The Gardens of Easter

Genesis 3:1–15; Mark 14:32–41;
John 19:38–41; 20:1–18 for children

Written by Joan Petersen Tietz
Illustrated by Barbara Kiwak

CONCORDIA PUBLISHING HOUSE • SAINT LOUIS

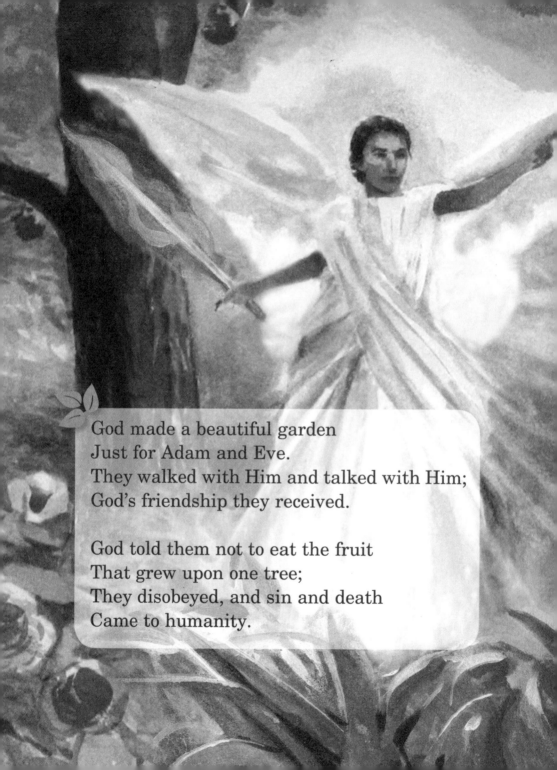

God made a beautiful garden
Just for Adam and Eve.
They walked with Him and talked with Him;
God's friendship they received.

God told them not to eat the fruit
That grew upon one tree;
They disobeyed, and sin and death
Came to humanity.

God told them to leave this garden;
It seemed they could not win.
But God promised to send His Son
To save us from our sin.

Then there was a peaceful garden
Where Jesus went to pray.
For the sins of humanity
His time had come to pay.

This place was called Gethsemane,
Where Jesus bowed and wept.
He prayed for strength and fortitude.
God's promises were kept.

And in that dark Gethsemane,
Our Savior was betrayed.
Soldiers came and arrested Him.
It had to be that way.

His enemies had done their job;
Jesus was convicted.
God's very own beloved Son
Would die, as was predicted.

Near the place of crucifixion,
There was a garden too,
Where our dear Savior Christ was laid
By friends whose heartache grew.

A stone was placed before His grave.
So heavy was this rock,
No one could go and take the Lord—
Now guarded round the clock.

Then women came to honor Him
Early on the third day,
But when they got to Jesus' tomb,
The stone was rolled away!

One woman ran away to tell:
The rock was moved away.
John and Peter looked in the tomb,
Saw angels there that day.

"Don't be afraid; your Lord has ris'n,"
The angels said to them.
It was just as He said before—
He died and rose again!

Mary went to the garden too,
Tears flowing from her eyes.
A man was standing right nearby,
The gard'ner—no surprise.

But then the man spoke just one word:
Her name so clear and true.
"Mary" was the name that He spoke.
The truth now Mary knew.

She turned around and cried "Teacher!"
Her grief now turned to joy!
She ran to tell the others too
That she had seen the Lord!

For on that cross, Christ died for us.
He takes our sins away.
Believe in Him, and you will live
With Him in heav'n one day.

Beyond the gardens of the earth,
A heav'nly garden grows—
A special place prepared for us.
Our names, the Savior knows.

Dear Parents,

While statistics vary, it's evident that more than half of all Americans are involved in some kind of gardening. The benefits of gardening can be physical, emotional, and financial. No one would deny that time spent in a beautifully tended garden brings a sense of peace and an appreciation for natural beauty.

Paradise, God's perfect creation, is described as a garden. Scripture links the Garden of Eden to heaven through fulfilled prophecy; it is in that garden where our heavenly Father promised that He would send a Savior, who would be the way to heaven.

As you experience the joyful Easter message with your child, start your own garden by planting some seeds outdoors if you can. If not, start a container garden indoors. Tell the message of Easter through these seeds. The seed is like the tomb. It appears to be lifeless. But God causes a plant to emerge from that seed, showing us new life!

Take a nature walk, and marvel at the beautiful spring flowers and plants that are in bloom. Talk about the miracle of each plant that God designed for a purpose and caused to grow. In the same way, God designed us for His purpose and causes our faith to grow through the words of our Lord and Savior, Jesus Christ.

The Author